AMERI-GEDDON

AMERI-GEDDON

Put Democracy Back
in the Hands of the People

FIRST EDITION

ALAN SUTTON
With Rex Yoshimoto

THE PEOPLE'S PRESS / Los Angeles

Cover design by Paradigm Shift Interactive

TPP

The People's Press

CONTENTS

The trouble with America is that when the dollar only earns 6% here, then it gets restless and goes overseas to get 100%. Then the flag follows the dollar and the soldiers follow the flag.

– Major General Smedley Butler

It is well enough that people of the nation do not understand our banking and monetary system, for if they did, I believe there would be a revolution before tomorrow morning.

– Henry Ford

A nation that continues year after year to spend more money on military defense than on programs of social uplift is approaching spiritual death.

– Martin Luther King, Jr.

These people are crazy.
– President John F. Kennedy, walking out of a 1961 meeting with top CIA and military advisors who wanted his authorization to use nuclear weapons.

AMERI-GEDDON

Put Democracy Back in the Hands of the People

Time to grab the pitchforks

In an age of waning democracy and political illiteracy, men and women of stunning mediocrity and depravity lead government today. Bought-and-paid-for by big business, their policies are wholly disconnected from the needs and aspirations of ordinary people.

The truly profound change of the twentieth century – the dominance of corporate power – has produced an equally profound change: the political demobilization of the citizenry.

After 30 years of a market-driven immorality, political corruption and a culture of cruelty and irresponsibility, the American public appears lifeless as it moves through a fog of civic illiteracy and unchecked greed and power.

Divide and conquer is the eternal law of authoritarian regimes. A disaggregated majority is a technique for dispersing popular power without repressing it. In America, if a 99% majority can't revive a hallmark democracy and a free-choice economy it will be for a lack of outrage at the corrupting power of money and the insolence of its elected representatives.

High time for the left and right to put aside our differences on peripheral issues and stand up to the billionaires and ethically-frozen politicians who preach the mutually related virtues of the free market and a permanent war economy.

(Authors' Note: The method of this pamphlet is descended from David Shields' literary manifesto, Reality Hunger *– a call-to-arms for a new creative code for the digital age: "Most of the passages in this book are taken from other sources. Nearly every passage I've clipped I've also revised, at least a little – for the sake of compression, consistency, whim." Herein likewise.)*

Power is a far more complex and mysterious quality than any apparently simple manifestation of it would appear. It is as much a matter of impression, of theatre, of persuading those over whom authority is wielded to collude in their subjugation.

Uncle Sam means business. Always on the march, doing sweetheart deals behind closed doors, he's hooked on making the supply-side dream come true. The dream here being give tax breaks to the wealthy and corporations, and wait for the money to trickle down. The less fashionable term being "voodoo economics." It's what you get when financial market engineering masquerades as sound economic policy. The consequence is a greedy and incompetent Wall Street free to unleash a tsunami of occult securities, drowning the world economy in uncontrollable debt and leaving taxpayers to pick-up the tab. Official Washington went along for the ride, flipping the bird to the middle class and allowing too big to fail to metastasize into too big to jail. Away from public view, the revolving door of the criminally insane in the Situation Room and Congress believe we can invade, bomb, drone, kill, occupy and tyrannize whomever we want, and that it is justified on the grounds of the general welfare.

> "As long as the priorities of those in government remain the interests of big business, rather than the people they were elected to serve, the impact of voting is negligible and it is our responsibility to be more active if we want real change. If more young people are talking about fracking rather than twerking we're heading in the right direction."
>
> – Russell Brand

Five years after the Global Financial Crisis democracy is under threat from plutocrats and politicians. Crony capitalism has perverted policy making and subverted free-market principles; the Supreme Court has decreed that corporations are people and money is free speech; corporations and lobbyists pay politicians big money to pass legislation that benefits them, not the American people; the president claims the right to serve as judge, jury and executioner of fellow citizens without due process; civil liberties are becoming an endangered species — all the while the illusion of freedom persists as the consent of the governed is manufactured using patriotic images and facts invented out of thin air, then efficiently relayed through the commercial media to anesthetize the public to reality. But populist movements such as the Tea Party and Occupy Wall Street aren't buying it. Could they be on to something?

Or is it all theatre: the contrived and empty productions of contemporary culture.

Today's American Society is the legacy of two liberation movements: the Woodstock generation revolt against soulless corporations and the military connection in the 1960s and the Reagan revolution against overweening government in the 1980s.

An extremely perilous development in U.S. politics: an alliance of energized right-wing populists with the most reactionary sector of Big Business has captured the Republican Party with the unabashed ambition to reverse decades of economic and social policy by any means necessary. They have embarked on an unprecedented overhaul of government on behalf of the one percent against all sectors of the poor and much of the working and middle classes, undermining the rights of all.

"Like most Americans I'm struggling just to get by, working hard and paying taxes. We all are angry at Uncle Sam's wallet-sucking schemes but too distracted chasing the elusive American Dream to do anything about it. Problem is, I hear timid squeaks rather than roof-top shouts. Hope they don't take away my SSI and veteran's disability...."

In one of the most astounding acts of legerdemain in US history, Republicans have convinced people that government – the only force capable of protecting us from the power of disproportionate wealth – is in fact, their enemy. The fat cats have conducted a silent coup to neuter the people and empower themselves while remaining largely invisible. Step one was to impoverish government and destroy people's faith in it; step two was to increase plutocratic power by increasing their role in the political process; and step three was to take over the media to make this explicit takeover invisible. Step one was accomplished by a massive investment in pseudo think tanks spewing counter-factual theories like "trickle down;" the strategic use of wedge issues; the creation of massive government debt by giving tax cuts (mostly to the rich); and a concerted effort to block any and all attempts to accomplish anything constructive. Step two was achieved by eliminating common-sense limits to campaign contributions and increasing corporate claims to personhood. Citizens United was the capstone of this effort. Step three was accomplished by eliminating the Fairness Doctrine – which required a station to present opposing points of view – and buying up media until it was largely controlled by mega corporations. At the end of

> "The value of political influence depends on our politicians' abilities to deceive the masses. Blatant special interest legislation must be hidden in a complex web to get it past the masses. But if we could expose instantly and efficiently the deception by our politicians, political deception would become essentially worthless. Big money won't buy something that doesn't work."
> – Carmen Yarrusso

the day, the only force that can trump this power of money is the power of people. Too bad we've been duped, fleeced and fooled into believing that government is inept, taxes are a curse and an uber-free market is our salvation.

In fact, there is a great deal one person working with others can do. Experiments across the country already focus on concrete actions that point toward a larger vision of long-term systemic change – especially the development of alternative economic institutions. Practical problem-solving activities on Main Streets across the country have begun to lay down the elements and principles of what might one day become the direction of a new system – one centered around building egalitarian wealth, nurturing democracy and community life, avoiding climate catastrophe and fostering liberty through greater economic security and free time.

Americans are so frustrated with government that responds only to the power of money; they want democracy to be renewed and made real. And they are using the tools afforded by the founders: the right to assemble and to petition for the redress of grievances. The key, now, is to do exactly what the progressive movement of a century ago and the civil rights and anti-poverty movements of 50 years ago did: we must turn the radical demands heard on the streets into radical demands at the ballot box and in the legislative process.

The wealthy have installed their slaves in the highest spheres of the state.

In the late 1960s and early 1970s, the corporate community, led by the U.S. Chamber of Commerce, became convinced that America was slipping out of its hands and the government was growing far too concerned with the needs of the poor and working class.* Ever since, corporations and the wealthy have devoted extraordinary resources to dominating the political process and the governance of the nation. They have succeeded, as the movement of both political parties to the right demonstrates. This movement to the right is not reflected by a shift in public opinion.

The Inner Circle was ensconced in the Pool Room at the Four Seasons, charged with delivering another banner year for militarized state capitalism, aka the "national interest." That the majority of the people are tired of endless war and seeing their country go down the tubes, means nothing to these captains of industry, career politicians, professional soldiers and their managed media collaborators. Answerable only to the financial gangsters who own and run America, they look down their noses

> "Today, the masters of the word are the masters of the world. They tell us that people who receive Social Security are to be reviled and their benefits must be cut because they are an entitlement. So too are free breakfasts for impoverished children and unemployment and welfare for those unable to find work in the Great Recession."
> – Ellen Dannin

*Elites in Europe and Japan were equally miffed, and with their American counterparts, produced a 1975 Trilateral Commission report on the governability of democracies titled The Crisis of Democracy. The report traced the problem to an "excess of democracy" in the wrong hands: workers, students, minorities, and intellectuals.

5

"Chomsky is a pretty neat guy. I listened to a CD of one of his live talks. Blew my mind, particularly his riff about 'reality' and the 'abuse of reality.' According to government propaganda, the myth that America can do no wrong is reality, while the actual historic record is merely the abuse of reality. Got that? Noam doesn't shake with the government bullies, so they try to hide him behind the 8 ball...

at the general population from the first class section of the gravy train.

K, veteran fixer for the high and mighty, was pontificating in a thick accent about the obligation of "the responsible men" to hold sway over the affairs of state. "The issues are much too important for the people to be left to decide for themselves," his face resembling a candle at mid-melt.

A small group of U.S. institutions select, groom, train, and certify a small number of individuals as exceptionally talented and warranting privilege. Bright prospects are passed along to think tanks, institutes, and centers.

There they learn the art of developing "policy proposals" and demolishing the arguments of their enemies. The tanks and centers function as ideological auxiliaries mobilized to promote the agendas favored by their sponsors. As an executive at one prominent think tank explained, "We're not here as some kind of Ph.D. committee giving equal time. Our role is to provide conservative public policy makers with arguments to bolster our side."

Alec, mouthpiece of the military-industrial-prison-financial cartel, reminded everyone of their marching orders – to advance the interests of their corporate masters and to claim at the same time that these efforts also serve the interests of the whole society. "We have a moral obligation to do what is right for the country," with a straight face, "and we must be ready to draw a line in the sand rather than compromise our core principles."

Joint Chiefs honcho Sheldon Jamison, his tongue loosened by frequent sips of Old No. 7, began to wonder out loud if MAD was an obsolete concept in the post 9-11 era. "We now have the ability to win a war without pulling any punches," striking his palm. "The decline in Russia's arsenal and the slow pace of modernization of China's nuclear forces, have created a situation in which neither could retaliate to our preemptive strike."

The US, a country with a vast nuclear weapons arsenal, whose political leaders are both corrupt and insane, is a great danger to life on earth. The criminal psychopaths in Washington have squandered trillions of dollars on their wars, killing and dispossessing millions of Muslims while millions of American citizens have been dispossessed of their homes and careers. Now the entire social safety net is on the chopping block so that Washington can finance more wars.

> "One of the problems in the world is that not enough people are frightened by the danger of nuclear war."
> – Nikita Krushchev

> "Nuclear weapons put everything we treasure at risk. These weapons and the strategies that sustain them are a suicide note to the planet. They are weapons capable of omnicide, the death of all."
> – David Krieger

Wall Street uses economic power backed by the threat of state power and the power of Western institutions like the IMF (International Monetary Fund) to insert itself into political economies around the globe and then restructure them for its own benefit. (For examples: see Goldman Sachs' currency swaps and their effect on Greek political economy or the effect of IMF "structural adjustment" programs in South America.) Through exploitative economic extraction based on naked power relationships Wall Street is both economically and politically destabilizing around the globe.

In fact it is highly probable that the 2008 financial crash was very carefully engineered to considerably weaken the world economy in order for the US to strengthen its control, which was cemented by heavily investing its public funds into the Wall Street banks that in fact form the core of its power.

Threats to U.S. financial hegemony by such as Saddam Hussein and Muammar Gaddafi to transfer payments for their raw energy products into the European Euro have been effectively and quickly resolved by their overthrow and elimination. (As Mike Whitney points out, "The dollar is the foundation upon which rests the three pillars of imperial strength: political, economic and military. Remove that foundation and the entire edifice comes crashing to earth.")

"21st century markets are much more powerful than any government," Wall Street bankster Winston Chisler, eager to get on with doing God's work. "Derivatives aren't called 'financial weapons of mass destruction' for nothing."

The most deadly weapons of mass destruction being used in the world today are not chemical or biological, they are the rules established by the World Trade Organization, the International Monetary Fund, the World Bank and the so-called free trade agreements that only escalate the levels of global inequality, human suffering and death.

Unknown to much of the public, Wall Street has been soaking state and municipal coffers with derivatives schemes and various frauds for years. Wallace Turbeville of the think tank Demos, referring to derivatives purchased by state and local governments, concludes that these municipalities would be better off hedging their risks by building a cash reserve, instead of paying the financial sector exorbitant fees for a product they don't understand.

"Every day I look up at the ceiling, wondering when the economic roof will collapse. The country is so broke from spending on Middle East wars; we're trillions of dollars in debt and have nothing to show for it. Already Russia, the Saudis and a host of Asian nations want to get paid in gold because they've lost faith in the US dollar. Tough luck: Fort Knox is out of stock....

As Michael Hudson has informed us, the goal of the financial sector has always been to convert all income, from corporate profits to government tax revenues, to the service of debt. From the bankers standpoint, the more debt the richer the bankers.

"If there is one thing both conservatives and liberals agree on, it is that the system is rigged against them," Chester South, a cable news windbag worth millions, interjected into the disjointed discussion. South was a hero to struggling whites who believe the economic stress they've experienced for decades is due to the government taking their money and giving it to the poor, who are disproportionately black and Latino. "What I would worry about is an alliance between the Tea Partiers and the Occupiers."

Alec had heard enough. "This isn't the fucking '60s," he spit. "Nowadays we have ways to prevent the wrong class of people from interfering with public affairs." (One of the reasons why "the sixties" continues to be a favorite punching bag of neocons and neoliberals is that it represented a decade of prolonged popular political education unique in recent American history.)

The general, too, was getting hot under the collar. "We have to maintain the strongest military on the planet," he fumed. "There is no alternative to spread freedom and prosperity."

For American elites one of the longest lasting and most powerful foreign policy goals has been preventing the rise of any society that might serve as a good example of an alternative to the capitalist model.

As the late former Central Intelligence Agency officer Phillip Agee has written, "The CIA, after all, is nothing more than the secret police of American capitalism, plugging up leaks in the political dam night and day so that shareholders of US companies operating in poor countries can continue enjoying the rip-off."

The task of elitism in the so-called age of democracy was not to resist democracy but to accept it nominally and then to set about persuading majorities to act politically against their own material interests and potential power.

"The conscious and intelligent manipulation of the organized habits and opinions of the masses is an important element in democratic society. Those who manipulate this unseen mechanism of society constitute an invisible government which is the true ruling power of our country," Edward Bernays, the father of modern public relations, telling it like it is in *Propaganda.*

The intense pace of work and the extended working day, combined with job insecurity, is a formula for political demobilization, for privatizing the citizenry. It works indirectly. Citizens are encouraged to distrust their government and politicians; to concentrate upon their own interests; to begrudge their taxes; and to exchange active involvement for symbolic gratifications of patriotism, collective self-righteousness, and military prowess. Above all, depoliticization is promoted through society's being enveloped in an atmosphere of collective fear and of individual powerlessness: fear of terrorists, loss of jobs, the uncertainty of pension plans, soaring health costs, and rising education expenses.

Why do so many Americans vote against their economic and social interests? Thomas Frank has an answer to this riddle in *What's The Matter With Kansas?*

"People getting their fundamental interests wrong is what American political life is all about. This species of derangement is the bedrock of our civic order; it is the foundation on which all else rests.

"This derangement is the signature expression of the Great

Backlash, a style of conservatism that first came snarling onto the national stage in response to the partying and protests of the late sixties. While earlier forms of conservatism emphasized fiscal sobriety, the backlash mobilizes voters with explosive social issues – summoning public outrage over everything from busing to un-Christian art – which it then marries to pro-business economic policies. Cultural anger is marshaled to achieve economic ends.

"I was riding with a bunch of wounded warriors to the VA hospital and some Iraqi vet was saying it's all an Illuminati plot – 9/11, the Great Recession, global warming, you name it. I'm not too familiar with underworld politics, but I know one thing: government keeps taking away our freedoms. Eventually people are going to strike back. It's no longer a matter of if, but when...

"Here is a movement whose response to the power structure is to make the rich even richer; whose answer to the inexorable degradation of working-class life is to lash out angrily at labor unions and liberal workplace-safety programs; whose solution to the rise of ignorance in America is to pull the rug from under public education."

Robert Reich, former Clinton Administration Labor Secretary, adds: "Guns, abortion, and race are part of the explanation. But don't overlook economic anxieties that translate into a willingness to vote for whatever it is that industry wants... People are so desperate for jobs they don't want to rock the boat. They don't want rules and regulations enforced that might cost them their livelihoods. For them, a job is precious – sometimes even more precious than a safe workplace or safe drinking water....This may explain why Republican officials who have been casting their votes against unions, against expanding Medicaid, against raising the minimum wage, against extended unemployment insurance, and against jobs bills that would put people to work, continue to be elected and re-elected. They obviously have the support of corporate patrons who want to keep unemployment high and workers insecure because a pliant working class helps their bottom lines. But they also, paradoxically, get the votes of many workers who are clinging so desperately to their jobs that they're afraid of change and too cowed to make a ruckus... The best bulwark against corporate irresponsibility is a strong and growing middle class. But in order to summon the political will to achieve it, we have to overcome the timidity that flows from economic desperation. It's a diabolical chicken-and-egg conundrum at the core of American politics today."

> "America's political class has been bought by Wall Street bankers with an efficiency and cynicism not seen since Cosimo de Medici bought up the 15th century papacy."
>
> – John Plender

> "If elites continue to fail, we will go on watching the rise of angry populists. The elites need to do better. If they do not, rage may overwhelm us all."
>
> – Martin Wolf

Policy making and financial elites have been discredited by their failed response to 9-11 and the Great Recession. With near-unanimous support in Congress and the mainstream media, the U.S.' unprovoked attack and occupation of Afghanistan and Iraq in the name of fighting global terrorism unleashed bloody sectarian violence throughout the Middle East, inflamed international jihadism and undermined America's image around the world – at a cost of trillions of dollars that could gone toward providing a better life for working people here at home.

Having brought the world economy to the precipice, globalized economic and financial elites were rewarded with trillions of dollars in government bailouts while millions of citizens lost their jobs and homes. The rescue may have been necessary. But the belief that the powerful sacrificed taxpayers to the interests of the guilty is correct.

If the corporate politicians have no answers, it is natural that the voters will look elsewhere.

Journalism is at a momentous crossroads. The alternative to unrelenting independence is sheepism, and that's not journalism; it's a professional baseline of bowing to government and corporate pressure even before it has been overtly exerted.

From the false Tonkin Gulf narrative in 1964 that boosted the Vietnam War to the fabricated baby-incubators-in-Kuwait tale in 1990 that helped launch the Gulf War to the reports of Iraqi weapons of mass destruction early in this century, countless deaths and unfathomable suffering have resulted from the failure of journalists to challenge falsehoods in high government places. The key problems, as usual, revolve around undue deference to authority, resulting in a huge loss of lives and a tremendous waste of resources that should be going to sustain human life rather than destroy it.

"Reagan said government is the problem, a maxim that has become holy writ not only among those on the Right, but among too many Democrats, as well as idiots in the 'news' media whose desperation for 'balance' leads them to accept and broadcast demonstrably disproven and discredited arguments."
– William Rivers Pitt

Democracy and accountable government simply do not exist when the executive branch can take a country to wars on behalf of secret agendas operating behind cover stories that are transparent lies. A government that will destroy the constitutional protections of free speech and a free press in order to protect its criminal actions from being disclosed is a tyrannical government.

Official Washington and the mainstream U.S. news media have learned nothing from the Iraq War debacle. Timely skepticism on matters of war and peace remain marginalized in small-circulation web sites with very few financial resources.

The role of independent media is to tell the truth about things that matter. That's quite different from the task of the commercial media. The mainstream media focuses on the food fight – who's winning the PR wars and who's losing – instead of the substantive issues, and as a result, democracy is being subverted.

Independent journalism is about to ascend to a whole new level of capability and influence with the establishment of First Look Media. Pierre Omidyar, the billionaire philanthropist and founder of eBay, has assembled for his new mass media organization a Murderer's Row of freelance journalists under the leadership of feisty muckraker Glenn Greenwald, who joins forces with Laura Poitras and Jeremy Scahill.

Their "personal brand journalism" and stalwart reputations, coupled with the lack of institutional constraints, will enhance the venture's chances for success. "I want to find ways to convert mainstream readers into engaged citizens," said Omidyar, who was approached about buying the Washington Post (now owned by Amazon.com CEO Jeff Bezos) of his vision for First Look. "I have always been of the opinion that the right kind of journalism is a critical part of our democracy."

"I just got off a website about how the USA is turning into a police state. It said the National Defense Authorization Act authorizes the military, under presidential authority, to arrest, kidnap, detain without trial and hold indefinitely American citizens thought to 'represent an enduring security threat to the United States.' Unless the Supreme Court overturns the law, we'll all be turning Japanese...

Added Greenwald, "After all these years of toiling on these issues, I'm thrilled to have a loud platform to warn of the dangers of state surveillance, US militarism, and government secrecy, and to herald the importance of individual privacy, internet freedom, and transparency for the world's most powerful factions. The people we have hired and will continue to hire – and, ultimately, the journalism we produce – will speak volumes about exactly the reasons we're doing this and why I'm so excited about it."

"When all three branches of the government are colluding against the interests of the people, it's the responsibility of journalists and journalism at large to hold them accountable," according to Scahill.

First Look Media has its work cut out for it. As journalism professor Jay Rosen notes, support from a "strong legal team" will be essential "because the kind of journalism (First Look) intends to practice is the kind that is capable of challenging some of the most powerful people in the world."

Real journalism is "subversive" of deception that can't stand the light of day. This is a huge problem for the Obama administration and the many surveillance-state flunkies of both parties in Congress. What they want is fake journalism, deferring to government storylines and respectful of authority even when it is illegitimate.

Business leaders and their elected friends fear workers' rage and resentment, should they be able to identify who and what did them in.

The Lehman Brothers crisis triggered a surge of popular anger against wealthy elites; hence the rise of the Tea Party, Occupy Wall Street.

There's a huge resentment on the far right and the far left, which actually extends quite a bit toward the middle of average Americans, that Wall Street screwed us and then bought off Washington – and got away with it.

For the last ten years, according to a new report by the Economic Policy Institute, the failure of the economy to provide a living wage to a majority of its workers has created a decade of stagnation. The cause of the situation, according to the report, began just as Ronald Reagan was about to be ushered into power in 1979 and is the result of intentional policy decisions – including globalization, deregulation, weaker unions and lower labor standards such as a weaker minimum wage – that have undercut job quality for low- and middle-wage workers. These policies have all been portrayed as giving American consumers goods and services at lower prices, but their real impact has been to cut earning power and upward mobility while making widely shared prosperity an impossibility.

What is wrong with the economy is not something no one can control – a giant meteor, bad weather, panic in the markets – but

> "At a time when income inequality is rising, it is little wonder that delegates have fretted about 'social cohesion' this week at Davos; nor that business executives have expressed concerns about populism. It is possible to imagine a scenario: that populism and social divisions rise, intensifying the risk of capricious state action."
> – Gillian Tett

something that most assuredly can and indeed should be, like the systemic transfer of wealth from the poor and middle-class to the rich that has characterized the class divide in Western nations since the 1970s. The appropriate, intelligent and self-preserving response to mass theft is rage, demands for action, and decisive punishment of political and economic leaders who refuse to change things.

A left-right alliance is extremely threatening to the establishment. A major way they keep principled progressives and conscientious conservatives hating instead of dialoguing is by not acknowledging all they have in common.

In fact, it would be perfectly possible to set up a broad Left-Right coalition of people opposed to militarism and interventionism. Of course, within the coalition, people may still disagree on gay marriage but, important as this issue may be, it should perhaps not prevent us from working together on other important issues, such as world peace, the defense of the UN and of international law, and the dismantling of the U.S. empire of bases.

Tom Ashbrook, host of NPR's On Point, has noted: "Ron Paul, '08 GOP presidential contender, is a conservative libertarian leading light and a Tea Party hero. Barney Frank is a no-apologies liberal Democrat. They agree on one big thing. America's giant military budget must be cut, in a giant way: a trillion dollar cut over the next decade."

"Apathy is a disease. We've become like frogs in hot water; as long as our freedoms are taken away incrementally, we pay no mind until it's too late. If you ask me, that's exactly what the government and the corporations want. They don't want people to band together with one voice like we did in the '60s. They're doing their best to keep us apart. The truth-tellers are called 'traitors' and jailed, or go underground. Where is the outrage, the catalyst for action?...

Economic populism is another right-left rallying point. With the top 1% pocketing fully 95% of the income growth of the society, working people want to be able to capture a fair share of the profits and productivity they help to produce. They demand Wall Street accountability and a curb on corporate power and trade deals that due great harm to workers rights and the environment.

The emerging awareness seems spreading among millennials, who are entering the worst jobs market since the Great Depression as companies employ their multi-trillion dollar cash hoard to buy-back stock and increase dividends rather than invest in growth and hiring. The young don't for a moment buy Washington's attack on Social Security and Medicare under the guise of protecting them from their greedy parents and grandparents. They get that public policy bears much of the blame for their economic difficulties.

On issue after issue – taxes, the environment, education, privacy, media control, drug policy – people understand that entrenched interests fix the game and feed off the public trough. They want to get health care costs under control not by cutting Medicare, but by taking on the drug and insurance companies and hospital complexes that make our health care costs twice those of other industrialized countries. They want an end to subsidies for Big Oil. They would end the tax breaks enjoyed by multinationals that ship jobs or report profits abroad. They would insure that billionaires pay higher taxes than their secretaries. And then use the money to pay for good public education for all children, to make college affordable, to be serious about advanced training for workers.

More than anything, they want less spending on defense so the programs and services we need are not devastated on the altar of deficit reduction.

America's Tea Party is a rising of the socially conservative poor, funded by the rich.

Tea Partiers, like many Americans, face declining incomes and a growing dread about their financial security. Inevitably, they scapegoat others. That does not mean their fears are imaginary. The Tea Party speaks for tens of millions of mostly non-urban whites, mostly middle-aged and older, who believe Mr. Obama is redistributing their hard-earned nest eggs to younger, less deserving, Americans. Their embittered sense of alienation has driven a selfish and destructive politics in Washington.

"What we have here is our core values as Americans and Christians slipping away into this facade where we should take care of our poor, sick, and disabled," Tea Party champion Ted Cruz said in the Senate during a one-hour speech that he gave in an attempt to block the funding of Obamacare. "It is disheartening to know that the nation our forefathers built is no longer of importance to our president and his Democratic counterparts. Not only that, we are falling away from core Christian values. I don't know about you, but I believe in the Jesus who died to save himself, not enable lazy followers to be dependent on him. He didn't walk around all willy-nilly just passing out free health care to those who were sick, or food to those who were hungry, or clothes to those in need. No, he said get up, brush yourself off, go into town

> "There's just one element missing from these snapshots of America's ostensibly spontaneous and leaderless populist uprising: the sugardaddies who are bankrolling it. Three heavy hitters rule… Rupert Murdoch and the Koch brothers, David and Charles. Their self- interested agendas go well beyond, and counter to, the interests of those who serve as spear carriers in the political pageants hawked on Fox News."
> – Frank Rich

23

and get a job, and as he hung on the cross he said, 'I died so that I may live in eternity with my Father. If you want to join us you can die for yourself and your own sins. What do I look like, your savior or something?' That's the Jesus I want to see brought back into our core values as a nation."

What does the Bible say about Sen. Cruz's "core Christian values?"

Matthew 25:41-45, "'Depart from me, you who are cursed, into the eternal fire prepared for the devil and his angels. For I was hungry and you gave me nothing to eat, I was thirsty and you gave me nothing to drink, I was a stranger and you did not invite me in, I needed clothes and you did not clothe me, I was sick and in prison and you did not look after me.' They will also answer, "Lord, when did we see you hungry or thirsty or a stranger or needing clothes or sick or in prison, and did not help you?' He will reply, 'I tell you the truth, whatever you did not do for one of the least among you, you did not do for me.'"

"Two politicians I really respected, Republican Rep. Paul Ryan and Democratic Sen. Patti Murray slammed the door in my face. Murray, a long time supporter of veterans, decided to cut-off our disability funds and pensions as part of their budget deal. That's why I'm a Tea Party prospect. I still have to check them out a little more. I don't want to be too close friends with Rush Limbaugh. Ha, ha....

Tea Partiers detest all things big: big government, big business, big national debt, big taxes. They express hostility toward the elite and outrage that the government has come to the aid of Wall Street while ignoring the plight of Main Street. Most Tea Partiers consider themselves citizen activists who are part of a grassroots movement that is organized from the bottom up – small groups united under a shared ideology.

Religiously sipping "the devil take the hindmost" brew of deep-pocketed Washington, D.C.-based pseudo populist political front groups, Tea Party activists have been tricked into blaming those below them on the socioeconomic ladder for problems that were caused by those far above them.

What Tea Party activists have on their side is cheap get-out-the-vote technology, motivated volunteers, and enough past success to provide a roadmap for would-be candidates. Ironically, they keep sending members to the House and Senate who consistently vote against the interests of millions of people just like them.

The Tea Party caucus in Congress has no positive agenda. Their goals: shut down the government, end Medicare as we know it, restrict women's access to health care, privatize Social Security. They have made the U.S. a spectacle of bad government, economic recklessness, and moral insensitivity.

It has been said that patriotism is the last refuge of a scoundrel. Hypocrites sporting American flag lapel pins who want to prevent people from voting, shove ultrasounds into women's vaginas, tell people who they can marry and what they should believe can now pass themselves off as defenders of freedom.

Tea Party members – you've been bamboozled! Despite what Republicans might try to tell you, the overwhelming majority of taxpayer funds are not going to social safety net programs like unemployment insurance or food stamps. Instead they're going to prop up multi-billion dollar corporations and an out-of-control military industrial complex that's ballooning in size and power.

Be wary of individuals and groups attempting to co-opt your cause for their own fundraising purposes. Your anger is justified and your activism is commendable. But rather than wage a rearguard revolt against the welfare state and the sexual revolution, leverage your strength by bonding with Occupy Wall Street to unite millions of potential swing voters in a powerful voting bloc of working people.

Occupy Wall Street is a rising in America of the socially liberal middle class, hounded by the establishment.

The middle classes have been on the front lines of opposition to abuses of power, whether by authoritarian or democratic regimes. The challenge for them is to turn their protest movements into durable political change, expressed in the form of new institutions and policies. Occupy Wall Street protestors, who peacefully demonstrated in parks to call attention to economic inequality and corporate abuse, have been accused of treason and sedition and subjected to brutal suppression. Yet what was the result of their activity? A renewed public focus on the gulf that separates haves from have-nots and Wall Street crime.

For good or ill, the Occupy movements had no leadership, no organization, and no strategic vision. What they had was indignation, and it is a sure thing that indignation will erupt again; where there are causes in abundance, there are bound to be effects. Perhaps we will find, when they do, that the lesson has been learned; perhaps, in the next wave of revolt, people will understand that outrage without organization is blind – and doomed.

The success of the "new left" in the '60s was to be limited by the failure of college kids and blue-collar workers to get together politically. One reason was the presence of real, invisible class force fields in the way of communication between the two groups.

Later many activist groups demanded college degrees, with a Masters or Ph.D., if you wanted leadership. Working people, even veteran activists, were too often shunned by the learned ones. It had a great bearing on tactics and how effective the tactics were, and were not. Being leftist is hard enough work. One has to study a lot and know the issues, but it takes the wind completely out of people's sails if someone who studied War 101 overrides those who did not attend college, but had actually been in war. It was sad to be continually gut checked by party hard liners, or dogmatic intellectuals, or naive wannabe types, to see that your ideas were thought bourgeois, when you had got your head cracked the last few demonstrations while they were busy studying, or leading some steering committee...It is no fun for a working person to fight for justice, laying it all on the line, but to be lectured about "the workers" by someone whose Daddy, or Ivory Tower purchased their lecturing ways.

This moral superiority that is peculiar to the left is a great impediment to momentum. If their ideas had been expressed in plain speech, perhaps a thoughtful population would have warmed to the movement instead of turning a cold shoulder. (Part of Dickens' genius was his gift for taking the messages of the intelligentsia and presenting them in a way ordinary people could understand and feel.)

> "Occupy Wall Street. They remind me of the hippies. 'Make love not war'. Equality. Sit-in at Murphy Hall, UCLA. That's O.K. They should merge with the Tea Party and create some long term goals, so their kids don't have to make a career out of driving a VW bus around Yellowstone. Focus on things they have in common, like stopping wars. Time out! You think Big Brother is trying to scrape me off the bottom of his shoe? Heh, heh...."

The conservative era will be brought to a close only through some kind of mass social movement on the left. But what kind of movement might succeed? Well, for one thing, a movement whose core values arise not from an abstract hostility to the state or from the need of protestors to find their voice but rather from the everyday lives of working people.

What should the Left do? First of all, mind its own business, which means struggling at home. And struggling for what? Peace through demilitarization of the West, a non-interventionist policy and putting diplomacy, not military threats, at the center of international relations.

The question that remains is how politics can be redefined through a new language that is capable of articulating not only what has gone wrong in the United States but also how the forces can be challenged in new ways by new social formations and collective movements.

Occupiers – your gutsy insurgency and message that another world is possible has inspired many across the world to become politically conscious and fight back against the forces of corporate capitalism. But there is more to be done to effect real change. Start by expanding your base by creating an alliance across socio-economic lines with the Tea Party. This would unite millions of potential swing voters into a powerful voting bloc ahead of the 2016 presidential election and beyond.

Structural factors in the U.S. election system and the influence of money have helped the Republicans and Democrats to remain the dominant parties in government for more than 150 years.

Before votes are ever counted, money determines the outcome of elections. It acts as a gatekeeper. Excluded from ballots, and debates, third party candidates with millions of supporters are effectively barred from participating. Millions of supporters matter less than millions of dollars.

Yet polls say a majority of voters are sick of both parties, want the incumbents out. Americans want more done on jobs. They want higher taxes for the wealthy and corporations. They want more educational opportunity, more social mobility, and more confidence in their economic future. These are policy planks that win.

Amid the latest government shutdown, 60% of Americans say the Democratic and Republicans parties do such a poor job of representing the American people that a third major party is needed. That is the highest Gallup has measured in the 10-year history of this question. A new low of 26% believe the two major parties adequately represent Americans.

A study titled "Testing Theories of American Politics: Elites, Interest Groups and Average Citizens" by Martin Gilens and Benjamin I. Page, adds fuel to the fire: "...America's claim to being a democratic society are seriously threatened...the preferences of the average American appear to have only a minuscule, near-zero, statistically non-significant impact upon public policy."

"As spontaneous, unpredictable movements reshaping the political landscape, the Tea Party and Occupy Wall Street have more in common than meets the eye. The parallels are much stronger than either prefers to admit."
– Jacob Weisberg

Elites, on the other hand, get their way virtually all of the time. "When a majority of citizens disagrees with economic elites and/or with organized interests, they generally lose. Moreover, because of the strong status quo bias built into the U.S. political system, even when fairly large majorities of Americans favor policy change, they generally do not get it."

Even the most ardent political foes agree on the need to abolish the morally bankrupt two-party system with its addiction to war, fossil fuel, globalization, NSA spying and dismantling the social safety net. A third major party will provide voters of all persuasions – Democrat, Republican, Independent, left and right – an alternative to the best democracy money can buy.

To become powerful enough to transform an unjust system, and push for reforms that benefit the great majority of working people in this country, history teaches us that a tactical use of electoral politics is necessary. With both the Democratic and Republican parties remaking the social landscape according to corporate interests we need a real political party representing our own needs and demands. The party has to represent a populist movement that grows out of a significant grassroots struggle. To assure this connection, candidates must run independent of the Republicans and Democrats.

Obamacare is an over-inflated moneyball. The Affordable Care Act...ha! If you purchase coverage, it costs twice as much as what you had. If you don't sign-up, the government will fine you and make you buy it anyway. Maybe the whole thing is doomed to fail, just like that retrograde website, which would leave single payer as the only real alternative to the current system of gouge and deny. If only....

With the 2016 presidential election still nearly two-and-a half years away there has never been a better time for the 99% to mount a challenge to the status quo. But it's no slam dunk.

In addition to the institutional barriers mentioned above, the third party movement will have to overcome the left's ideological split when it comes to elections.

"On the left, it has long been argued whether electoral politics can have any lasting effect on societal change or whether activists should instead focus solely on building social movements. In the latter camp, commentators... argue that a run for president by Bernie Sanders, for example, would be a huge waste of time and resources, and some even call for boycotts of elections... The argument goes that even electoral movements independent of the two-party system, such as the Green Party, weaken popular movements by pacifying them and quickly devolve into duopoly politics as usual," Green Party member Michael Trudeau, reflecting on the left's political disarray.

> "The structures of the corporate state must be torn down. Its security apparatus must be destroyed. And those who defend corporate totalitarianism, including the leaders of the two major political parties, fatuous academics, pundits and a bankrupt press, must be driven from the temples of power. Main Street protest and prolonged civil disobedience are our only hope. A failure to rise up will see us enslaved. "
>
> – Chris Hedges

What movement purists are missing, according to electoral activists, is that alternative party-building poses a serious challenge to the corporatocracy. Democrats and Republicans worry about third parties threatening their rule. Why else would they routinely pass bipartisan legislation meant to thwart the advancement of alternative parties?

As long as Washington is a protection racket for the 1%, the Tea Party and Occupy Wall Street movements are wasting their energy backing Republicans and Democrats. Instead they should focus on all they have in common and start a third major party.

"In real communities in real places across the United States, I've found that liberals and conservatives share many of the same concerns and problems and simply gravitate toward two different sides in searching for solutions," CNN contributor Sally Kohn on her previous stint as a progressive talking-head on Fox News.

To take on the plutocracy, the Tea Party and Occupy Wall Street need to show respect for each other's opinions, even when they disagree, and work together to solve the most pressing problems facing ordinary Americans: perpetual war, income inequality and environmental plunder.

Both movements draw their strength by rallying people who are sickened by the immorality of the status quo. Joining forces to create a third major party (for want of a better term, let's call it the 3rd Party for now) will enable them to channel their moral outrage into political power that challenges the institutions and policies that favor the few at the expense of the many. The obscenity of tax cuts for the wealthy and big corporations while cutting necessary public services is not just a misplacement of priorities, but immoral decisions.

"Reid, McCain, Boehner, McConnell – all the so-called leaders of Congress – they don't care about working people or society at large. Campaign donations are the only thing that matters to them, that and being on the speaking circuit. And nobody believes President snake-oil, a junior senator with a pedigree in community organizing, is calling the shots for the world's only superpower....

A left-right coalition can use its power-of-the-purse to demand a livable wage and an end to corporate domination of the national economy and politics. "Given how much taxpayers contribute to our nation's finances (46% of all federal income taxes, versus 13.5% from corporate income taxes), it goes without saying that we should be able to influence how the government spends the money," says Robert Claremont of Campaign for America's Future.

We know that we live in a populist moment. The unknown is whether a movement will grow to clean out Washington and make the government an instrument of the common good, rather than the private interest.

A 3rd Party run for president of the United States in 2016, one that represents a permanent alternative to the corrupt two-party system at the national level, would be revolutionary in American politics; tapping into the zeitgeist, it would trigger a bottom-up citizen movement to override the power of money and restore people's faith in government.

> "Both parties bow down before the free market, and loyally serve the interests of their masters – the only difference being a matter of degree. The political system is completely dysfunctional. It is drowning in corporate cash. Working people, youth, people of color, women, the elderly, the disabled, immigrants – the 99% –have no voice or representation. We need our own political party."
> – Kshama Sawant

As the Obama era nears its final midterm elections, the campaign to succeed him has already begun: Prospective candidates on both sides have begun quietly courting donors, taking steps to build an organization and making scouting trips to early voting states like Iowa, New Hampshire and South Carolina. The official starting line, however, is likely a year away. Meanwhile, both parties are involved in an intra-party power struggle with their populist wings – Tea Party Republicans and Elizabeth Warren-led Democrats. Coupled with the specter of midterm elections, it's unlikely that either side with get anything done.

Given the fractious state of U.S. politics it is possible to imagine the left and right coalescing around a third party movement for president in 2016.

Beginning with online activists and clever PR the 3rd Party phenomenon would gain a first mover advantage. Its populist vision of greater economic justice and working class influence in government can reinvigorate voters fed up with choosing between the lesser of evils – heartless Republicans or spineless Democrats.

While the establishment Candidates-in-Waiting focus on building the foundations of a campaign, compiling a policy agenda and raising money for House, Senate and gubernatorial candidates who could become future allies, the 3rd Party can steal a march by adopting a platform that meets the needs of ordinary Americans for well-paying jobs, affordable housing, a dignified retirement, equal educational opportunities and environmental protection.

In the interest of campaign finance reform, the 3rd Party campaign must not accept any corporate money. It should also refrain from using expensive TV commercials to sling mud at the opposition. Instead, its candidate for the highest office in the land (and his/her running mate) should hold a series of town hall meetings around the country to call attention to the substantive issues that normally don't get talked about amid the name calling and political posturing. These include:

• **Wall Street.** Why are we still doing business with a corrupt international banking cartel when the public banking option offers viable solutions to the present economic crisis in the U.S.? A public bank can create new jobs and spur economic growth, generate new revenues for states, lower debt costs for local governments, strengthen local banks and even out credit cycles and build up small businesses. Unlike private banks whose sole concern is maximizing profits, public banks are required to promote the public interest as defined in their charters.

• **War and peace.** Americans are exhausted after a decade of unsuccessful warfare. With a huge deficit and enormous unmet needs, it is absurd that the United States continues to spend almost as much on defense as the rest of the world combined. To redeem the meaning of America the U.S. must be the world's leader in nuclear disarmament and efforts toward peace, not in the sale of weapons of death and destruction.

"Social Security is an earned benefit. You've worked hard for it and paid taxes on it; it's your money. But the bureaucrats in Washington call it an 'entitlement,' which means they can take it away at any time. If you protest, they call you a bum, a moocher – and try to turn the youth against you, saying it's a Ponzi scheme that only benefits seniors and will go bust before they are eligible to collect....

• **Civil liberties.** Clearly, the National Security Agency (NSA) and some of the other intelligence agencies are out of control. We need to protect this country from terrorism, but we must do it in a way that does not undermine our constitutional rights.

• **Jobs and wages.** With both political parties worshipping on the altar of austerity, we need to reverse course and make significant investments in our crumbling infrastructure, in early childhood education and in affordable housing – spending that not only improves the quality of life in our country but also creates millions of decent-paying jobs. We also need to establish a progressive tax system which asks the wealthy to start paying their fair share of taxes. Finally, we need to raise the minimum wage to a living wage and expand efforts at worker-ownership of the places in which they work.

• **Retirement security.** For millions of Americans Social Security and Medicare are the only things keeping them from spending their twilight years in poverty. We must expand both of these successful New Deal programs and make sure that every American can retire with dignity.

• **Trade policy.** So-called "free trade" agreements such as NAFTA and pending Trans Pacific Partnership (TPP) and the Transatlantic Trade and Investment Partnership (T-TIP) have very little to do with trade. Rather, they are investor rights agreements with enforcement provisions that allow multinational companies to sue sovereign nations for economic damages due to policies that support labor, food safety and the environment. People power has proven effective in stalling negotiations on these agreements, which are undemocratically hammered out in secret, and citizen protests need to continue and grow.

• **Climate change.** Why are we still giving billions of dollars of subsidies to the fossil fuel industry? We need to combat global warming by investing in energy efficiency and sustainable energy instead of continuing to expand our reliance on environmentally risky energy sources such as hydraulic fracturing and nuclear power.

What America lacks is a figure with the serene self-confidence to tell us the twin idols of national security and corporate power are outmoded dogmas that have nothing more to offer us. Someone who can inspire change by motivating "25 million or so people vote for a radical non-corporate party in presidential elections, plus non-corporate candidates winning councils, state legislatures, and then seats in Congress, ensuring these social movements have the political legitimacy that should already be rightfully theirs," according to Trudeau's calculation.

To compete against the big money interests backing the establishment candidates, the Tea Party and Occupy Wall Street must strengthen their ground game. They will need to work with multiple existing third parties and create parties or ballots in states where there is not an existing third party. The Green Party will be on the ballot in half the states by 2016. There are also state-level progressive parties whose nominations should be sought, as well as smaller national parties. If their candidate is nominated by a coalition of parties, the 3rd Party will only have to get on the ballot of 20 or so more states.

"In recent elections, there has been a growing awareness of the unfairness of the private corporation that sponsors presidential debates," Kevin Zeese and Margaret Flowers, organizers of the peace and justice movement clearinghouse Popular Resistance, referring to the second major obstacle facing third party candidates. "This corporation, co-chaired by former leaders of the Republican and Democratic Parties and funded by big-business interests, has worked hard to keep third-party candidates out. The combination of (the 3rd Party candidate's) credibility and the movement challenging the Commission on Presidential Debates makes it possible to overcome this challenge."

If the 3rd Party's ballot drive and debate inclusion efforts are successful, its entry into the 2016 presidential race would be a world gone wild for the establishment. The corporate media, in

a flat-footed attempt to flex its agenda-setting muscle – most likely fed by Third Way Democrats who blame Ralph Nader for Al
Gore's 2000 defeat – will frame the insurgency as being naïve and
disruptive. The two main parties will carpet bomb the airwaves
with negative ads to conceal their lack of solutions to the monu-
mental problems facing the country. Fed up with the opposition's
resort to personal attacks, voters will take a closer look at the 3rd
Party candidates' positions on the issues they care about – jobs and
income inequality, health care, education, the environment and
foreign policy.

When that happens, we may finally be able to break the Democrats' and Republicans' stranglehold on the White House.

Democracy is about the conditions that make it possible for ordinary people to better their lives by becoming political beings and by making power responsive to their hopes and needs.

The kind of democracy that now envelops us – with its billionaires and its unemployed millions, its surveillance state and its unelected technocrats, its individual gratification and its ever-narrowing visions of the collective good – is one that previous generations would have regarded as a nightmare.

No one who lives under constant surveillance, who is subject to detention anywhere at any time, whose conversations, messages, meetings, proclivities and habits are recorded, stored and analyzed, can be described as free. The relationship between the U.S. government and the U.S. citizen is now one of master and slave.

Full Medicare for all, cracking down on corporate abuses, a fairer tax system, a broad public works program, a living wage, access to justice and citizen empowerment, clean election practices, and pulling back on the expensive, boomeranging Empire to come to America's necessities and legitimate hopes are some examples of what the people want. But Washington has turned a deaf ear.

When a state-corporate nexus of power has bypassed democracy and made a mockery of the voting process, when an unreformed political funding system ensures that parties can be bought and sold, when politicians of the main parties stand and watch as public services are divvied up by a grubby cabal of privateers, what is left of the system that inspires us to participate?

That depends on what kind of a world and what kind of a society we want to live in, "in particular, in what sense of democracy do we want this to be a democratic society," Noam Chomsky on The Spectacular Achievements of Propaganda.

"The issue is whether we want to live in a free society or whether we want to live under what amounts to a form of self-imposed totalitarianism, with the bewildered herd marginalized, directed elsewhere, terrified, screaming patriotic slogans, fearing for their lives, and admiring with awe the leader who saved them from destruction, while the educated masses goose-step on command and repeat the slogans they're supposed to repeat and the society deteriorates at home. We end up serving as a mercenary enforcer state, hoping that others are going to pay us to smash up the world."

There is a new normal in America: our government may shut down, but our wars continue.

Americans across-the-board are fed up with war. Liberals, conservatives and independents – even libertarians and the paleoconservative Right – advocate a non-interventionist foreign policy. The ultimate solution to end wars is for the people to overthrown the reigning elites, who for more than a half century have presided over a militarized economic system that is the No. 1 terrorist threat to the future of humanity.

Yet, the U.S. military remains a powerful potential instrument of destruction, death, and destabilization, writes Tom Engelhardt. "In terms of advanced and unchallenged military power, there has been nothing like the U.S. armed forces since the Mongols swept across Eurasia. No other nation's military comes within a country mile of it:

- Its fleet, with 11 aircraft carrier battle groups, rules the seas and has done so largely unchallenged for almost seven decades.
- Its Air Force has ruled the global skies, and despite being almost continuously in action for years, hasn't faced an enemy plane since 1991 or been seriously challenged anywhere since the early 1970s.
- Its fleet of drone aircraft has proven itself capable of targeting and killing suspected enemies in the backlands of the planet from Afghanistan and Pakistan to Yemen and Somalia with little regard for national boundaries, and none at all for the possibility of being shot down.
- It funds and trains proxy armies on several continents and has complex aid and training relationships with militaries across the planet. On hundreds of bases, some tiny and others the size of American towns, its soldiers garrison the globe from Italy to

Australia, Honduras to Afghanistan, and on islands from Okinawa in the Pacific Ocean to Diego Garcia in the Indian Ocean.

- Its weapons makers are the most advanced on Earth and dominate the global arms market.

- Its nuclear weaponry in silos, on bombers, and on its fleet of submarines would be capable of destroying several planets the size of Earth.

- Its system of spy satellites is unsurpassed and unchallenged. Its intelligence services can listen in on the phone calls or read the emails of almost anyone in the world from top foreign leaders to obscure insurgents.

- The CIA and its expanding paramilitary forces are capable of kidnapping people of interest just about anywhere from rural Macedonia to the streets of Rome and Tripoli.

- For its many prisoners, it has set up (and dismantled) secret jails across the planet and on its naval vessels.

- It spends more on its military than the next most powerful 13 states combined. Add in the spending for its full national security state and it towers over any conceivable group of other nations.

"The chicken hawks keep sending our children to fight endless wars in order to protect their profitable overseas interests. Stop and think for a minute. Can you honestly say we're fighting to spread freedom and liberty, or to keep our country safe? When your bright, innocent kid comes home without eyes, ears, arms and legs, they yank his benefits and give him a pencil cup for his service. That, is Bravo Sierra....

"Despite this stunning global power equation, for more than a decade we have been given a lesson in what a military, no matter how overwhelming, can and (mostly) can't do in the twenty-first century... "Washington's military plans and tactics since 9/11 have been a spectacular train wreck...

"But our leaders' faith in war remains remarkably unbroken in a century in which military power has become the American political equivalent of a state religion."

If it weren't for the Tea Party's vehement opposition (along with Russia), the U.S. would probably be dropping bombs on Syria right now, and very possibly sinking deeper into prolonged military involvement there.

Stop counting carrier fleets, fighter jets and cruise missiles. America's wars in Iraq and Afghanistan showed the limits of military might. Today's great games revolve around another dimension of power. Geopolitics is making way for Geoeconomics.

That should be good news for American workers, the most skilled and productive in the world. The only thing holding them back is the reigning elites. For undermining the economy in their quest to dominate world markets by force, they must be shown the door. And for squandering the Peace Dividend, they need to make reparations to the American people.

The collapse of the Soviet Union presented Washington with the grand opportunity to reallocate the Pentagon budget to other uses. Part of the reduction could have been returned to taxpayers for their own use. Another part could have been used to improve worn out infrastructure. And another part could have been used to repair and improve the social safety net, thus insuring domestic tranquility. A final, but perhaps most important part, could have been used to begin repaying the Treasury IOUs in the Social Security Trust Fund from which Washington has borrowed and spent $2 trillion, leaving non-marketable IOUs in the place of the Social Security payroll tax revenues that Washington raided in order to fund its wars and current operations.

> "It is no accident that the defense contractors spread work on the hugely expensive – and problem-plagued – F22 jet fighter program across 46 states and a majority of congressional districts. Most of the time, the Pentagon colludes with Congress to perpetuate the waste and duplication."
> – Edward Luce

Instead, influenced by neoconservative warmongers who advocated America using its "sole superpower" status to establish hegemony over the world, Washington let hubris and arrogance run away with it. The consequence was that Washington destroyed its soft power with lies and war crimes, only to find that its military power was insufficient to support its occupation of Iraq, its conquest of Afghanistan, and its financial imperialism.

> "Labor has always been in the crosshairs of big business and its hired goons in Congress. Whether it's blocking union organizing efforts, not raising the minimum wage or passing fraudulent 'free trade' agreements that ship formerly good paying jobs overseas, politicians will always side with their corporate paymasters. D.C. needs a thorough housecleaning – as well as a strong disinfectant ...

Taxpayers are on the hook for trillions of dollars that go towards propping up the permanent war economy. Among the main beneficiaries are the big banks. Relentlessly sucking blood money from Uncle Sam's wars, they are raking in billions more from market-based trading that creates huge profits without producing anything.

"War, for big business, has always been very lucrative and used as an excuse to curtail basic liberties and crush popular movements,' Chris Hedges on the dark side of corporate America. "The horror of September 11th was masterfully manipulated by the security state and our for-profit military-industrial complex. These forces used the attacks as an excuse to increase the massive pilfering of taxpayer dollars."

Adds Mike Whitney, "For some unknown reason, America's behemoth oil corporations think the resources that lie beneath Russian soil belong to them. The question is whether their agents will push Obama to put American troops at risk to assert that claim. If they do, there's going to be a war."

Without a change in foreign policy we'll get dragged into more unnecessary wars. And the economic fallout will be the least of our worries.

Ordinary folks, the 99%, don't have money anymore, Mr. President. The rich 1% and corporations do.

The super rich want the homeless to get jobs. But they don't want to pay taxes to support job creation. If the richest Americans – the Forbes 400 – had paid a 5% tax on their 2012 investment earnings, enough revenue would have been generated to provide a full time minimum wage job for every person who was homeless in America on a January night in 2012.

With the "financialization" of the economy and the adoption of neoliberalism as the preferred model of economic governance, financial markets begin to dominate economic decision making processes and the financial elite exercise enormous influence on government policies...Decisions about the future direction of the economy are political in nature and highly antidemocratic. Labor's voice is totally ignored. Privatizing profits and socializing losses reigns supreme.

In January 2013 Fix the Debt (the $40 million AstroTurf supergroup) steering committee member and former Tennessee Governor Phil Bredesen admitted that Fix the Debt's strategy was to create an "artificial crisis" to achieve a "grand bargain" on Medicare and Social Security.

> "The multiple decades of regulation assassination, the combining of financial services from insurance policies to our pension funds, the epic leverage in the banking system, the enabling of the derivatives market to reach many times the world's GDP – are all time bombs of financial devastation...They bet most legislators (excluding Bernie Sanders and Elizabeth Warren) will focus anywhere else."
> – Nomi Prins

Americans are very clear. They don't want people screwing around with their retirement and they don't believe in these grand bargains.

The so-called grand bargain – a chickenshit political slogan if ever there was one – is another wealth-transfer-upward scheme. At a time when the chickens are coming home to roost, when the floating craps game known as free market capitalism has wiped out the poor and much of the working and middle class, the wealthy must be made to understand that today's obscene levels of inequality are also destabilizing the global political economy.

Perhaps being called out by one of their own will do the trick.

"Now it's time to share some of your good fortune by paying higher taxes or reforming them to favor economic growth and labor as opposed to corporate profits and individual gazillions," PIMCO's Bill Gross, to the "Scrooge McDucks" of the world.

Most of the poverty in the United States is artificially manufactured. The financial pundits feign bewilderment as to why QE has had a negligible impact on business investment and job creation, despite the Fed's stated goal of stimulating the economy and reducing unemployment. As they should well know, the Fed's multi-trillion-dollar bond purchase scheme was not intended to boost the economy, but rather was a desperate Hail Mary pass designed to keep the banks solvent by preventing a catastrophic decline in value of their unregulated $1 quadrillion derivatives books.

As former Federal Reserve official Andrew Huszar recalls, "I was responsible for executing the centerpiece program of the Fed's first plunge into the bond-buying experiment known as quantitative easing. The central bank continues to spin QE as a tool for helping Main Street. But I've come to recognize the program for what it really is: the greatest backdoor Wall Street bailout of all time. Despite the Fed's rhetoric, my program wasn't helping to make credit any more accessible for the average American. The banks were only issuing fewer and fewer loans. More insidiously, whatever credit they were extending wasn't getting much cheaper. QE may have been driving down the wholesale cost for banks to make loans, but Wall Street was pocketing most of the extra cash.

Having racked up hundreds of billions of dollars in opaque Fed subsidies, U.S. banks have seen their collective stock price triple since March 2009. The biggest ones have only become more of a cartel: 0.2% of them now control more than 70% of the U.S. bank assets. As for the rest of America, good luck."

Most bank lending today does not create value-added but volatility and debt burdens. Let's face it: banks hinder and hurt the economy more than they help it.

Business tax cuts don't create many jobs any longer since, in a global economy, they are easily diverted offshore or into financial investments by corporations today; or used to buy back stocks, pay dividends, retire debt; or just hoarded as retained earnings in offshore tax havens or in companies' foreign subsidiaries.

Big business and finance capital are using the debt crisis as an opportunity to dismantle the social state, to sell off profitable public enterprises and state assets at bargain prices, to deprive labor of even its most basic rights after decades of hard-fought struggles against management, and to substantially reduce wages and rob pensions.

The economy is a system of rules, and we can change the rules if we are mobilized. Anyone who says you have to cut taxes to promote growth doesn't know history.

Our adventure on Earth is imperiled, and should man persist in making the planet uninhabitable it will come to an end.

"The case I want to make to you is that climate change – when its full economic and moral implications are understood – is the most powerful weapon progressives have ever had in the fight for equality and social justice," the unswervingly prescient Naomi Klein.

We are in the midst of economic, social and environmental crises, with global warming looming larger. We are also threatened by pollution, natural resource degradation, loss of forests and biodiversity, as well as socio-political instability due to growing disparities.

When scientists at Mauna Loa Observatory on the big island of Hawaii recently announced that global CO_2 emissions had crossed a threshold at 400 parts per million (ppm) for the first time in millions of years, a sense of dread spread around the world and not only among climate scientists.

According to new research, the debate over whether climate change is real, even in the Conservative heartland, is over. A new study from Stanford University shows that even among the nation's most right-wing constituencies the debate about whether or not climate change is happening is over. Research headed by Professor Jon Krosnick, a social psychologist who studied years

"In the US, extreme weather – as we have already seen with Hurricanes Katrina and Sandy – will disproportionately affect economically fragile areas, made up of marginalized communities: indigenous people, people of color, immigrants, the elderly, LGTB people. Climate activists will need to build alliances around these diverse issues, and listen to, and lift up, the voices of disenfranchised people."
– Jose-Antonio Orosco

worth of polling data to reach his conclusions, found that even in the reddest political states, like Texas and Oklahoma, a majority of people not only believe that climate change is negatively impacting their environment but they actually want the government to step in to fix the problem. "To me, the most striking finding that is new today was that we could not find a single state in the country where climate skepticism was in the majority," Krosnick said.

Carbon concentrations have not been this high since the Pliocene period, between 3 million and 5 million years ago, when global average temperatures were 3°C or 4°C hotter than today, the Arctic was ice-free, sea levels were about 40m higher and jungles covered northern Canada; Florida, meanwhile, was under water along with other coastal locations we now call New York, London, Shanghai, Hong Kong, Sydney and many others. Crossing this threshold has fuelled fears that we are fast approaching converging "tipping points" – melting of the subarctic tundra or the thawing and releasing of the vast quantities of methane in the Arctic sea bottom – that will accelerate global warming beyond any human capacity to stop it.

"Big corporations hype their token civic and charitable activities to divert attention from how they wreck the environment. They saturate Public Broadcasting with sappy commercials about giving books and computers to schools, or supporting state construction projects – everything to counseling unwed mothers and feeding hungry orphans. It hides their real agenda, but corporately that's how we roll...

The world's climate scientists tell us we're facing a planetary emergency. They've been telling us since the 1990s that if we don't cut global fossil fuel greenhouse gas emissions by 80-90% below 1990 levels by 2050 we will cross critical tipping points and global warming will accelerate beyond any human power to contain it. Yet despite all the ringing alarm bells, no corporation and no government can oppose growth and, instead, every capitalist government in the world is putting pedal to the metal to accelerate growth, to drive us full throttle off the cliff to collapse.

We all know what we have to do: suppress greenhouse gas emissions. Stop over-consuming natural resources. Stop the sense-less pollution of the earth, waters, and atmosphere with toxic chemicals. Stop producing waste that can't be recycled by nature. Stop the destruction of biological diversity and ensure the rights of other species to flourish. We don't need any new technological breakthroughs to solve these problems. Mostly, we just stop doing what we're doing.

> "We've always been living on borrowed time. Getting away cheap. Never caring about who's paying for it, who's starving somewhere else all jammed together so we can have cheap food, a house, a yard in the burbs...planetwide, more every day, the payback keeps gathering."
>
> – Thomas Pynchon

This doesn't mean we would have to de-industrialize and go back to riding horses and living in log cabins. But it does mean that we would have to abandon the "consumer economy" – shut down all kinds of unnecessary, wasteful and polluting industries from junkfood to cruise ships, disposable Pampers to disposable H&M clothes, disposable IKEA furniture, endless new model cars, phones, electronic games, the lot. Plus all the banking, advertising, junk mail, most retail, etc. We would have completely redesign production to replace "fast junk food" with healthy, nutritious, fresh "slow food," replace "fast fashion" with "slow fashion," bring back mending, alterations and local tailors and shoe repairmen. We would have to completely redesign production of appliances, electronics, house wares, furniture and so on to be as durable and long-lived as possible. Bring back appliance repairmen and such. We would have to abolish the throwaway disposables industries, the packaging and plastic bag industrial complex, bring back re-fillable bottles and the like. We would have to design and build housing to last for centuries, to be as energy efficient as possible, to be reconfigurable, and shareable. We would have to vastly expand public transportation to curb vehicle use but also build those we do need to last and be shareable like Zipcar or Paris' municipally-owned "Autolib" shared electric cars.

Finally, we have to press forward with nuclear disarmament and simultaneously demand that governments around the world learn from the catastrophe in Japan and decommission the ticking time bombs manufactured – and managed with criminal neglect – by the atomic energy industry.

The ongoing disaster at the Daichi Fukushima nuclear power plant will last for generations. The dangerous trajectory from nuclear weapons to nuclear power is now being challenged by a popular demand for peace and sustainability. It is a lesson for the rest of the world as well.

We may be fast approaching the precipice of ecological collapse, but the means to derail this train wreck are in the making as, around the world, struggles against the destruction of nature, against dams, against pollution, against overdevelopment, against the siting of chemical plants and power plants, against predatory resource extraction, against the imposition of GMOs, against privatization of remaining common lands, water and public services, against capitalist unemployment and insecurity are growing and building momentum.

As the War on Terror enters its second decade the state ceaselessly peddles economic and geopolitical fear to keep the population traumatized and immobilized.

The object is to create a climate in which people do not think of rebelling, a climate in which their dwindling faith in political institutions leads to a steady decline in voter participation rates. The perception takes hold that society is at the mercy of pitiless external forces – technology, globalization, bankers – and that they exert less influence than ever on the decisions of elites.

We all know the world is in big trouble. The Three Great Problems are: (1) incessant war and violence; (2) financial crisis provoking widespread economic suffering; (3) environmental degradation bordering on catastrophe.

Change often happens by making the brutality of the status quo visible and so intolerable. The situation everybody has been loving is suddenly described in a new way by a previously silenced or impacted constituency, or with new eloquence, or because our ideas of what is humane and decent evolve, or a combination of all three.

> "Arising from the hot molten fires of Id and libido, Ted Cruz emerges to (lead) the deluded toward an impossible fulfillment of their will and personal freedom, to lead The Many away from a democratic society and its institutions, away from a workable liberal democracy and deeper into self-absorbed fantasies that have no social value or concern."
> – Joseph Natoli

As the government's powers of surveillance grow, progressives will learn new respect for the conservative instinct that state power must be kept in check. As the globalization of finance multiplies the risk of systemic meltdown, conservatives will learn to accept that the state has to take care of the market's victims. And as the economic and human costs of perpetual war continue to escalate, both sides will demand a halt to foreign interventionism and instead focus on renewing the social contract to ameliorate the new economy's disadvantages for working people.

What is missing are those alternative public spheres, those cultural formations that can bring people together and embody those ideas that are important to their lives in both a sense of hope, of vision and the organizations and strategies that would be necessary at the very least to start a third party. To start a party that is not part of this establishment, to reconstruct a sense of where politics can go.

> "Regardless of their social views folks need to be raising hell, NOW, before the country is corporatized to the point of no return. Once the average working stiff looks beyond the beer can in his hand, sees who's really behind the theft of his liberty and livelihood, and takes out his anger at the voting booth, the rulers and their lackeys will be swept away in a landslide of their own bullshit."

The right since the 1970s has created a massive cultural apparatus, a slew of anti-public intellectuals. They've invaded the universities with think tanks. They have foundations. They have all kinds of money. The war they wage is a war on the mind. The war on what it means to be able to dissent, the war on the possibility of alternative visions. And the left really has – and progressives and liberals – have nothing like that. It always seems to believe that all you have to do is tell the truth.

The large social movements on the left have fragmented into isolated pockets of resistance mostly organized around a form of identity politics that largely ignored the much-needed conversation about the attack on the social and the broader issues affecting society such as the growing inequality in wealth, power and income. So far, their resistance to the deadly effects of predatory capitalism have had rather limited effect.

How to keep the issue of inequality and class in the foreground?

You have to ask for something that's big enough to mobilize people around. If we can't mobilize people, we can't move the agenda. So you need to ask for things that are popular. The obvious one is to have minimum-wage events everywhere. It's popular, and it fits in with all the organizing that's going on at the grassroots. The minimum wage is a place where we could help define ourselves in a way that fits in with everything else we care about – and it's popular.

In the past few months, American voters have approved higher minimum wages by hefty margins. California and Massachusetts recently took it over $10 an hour – way ahead of the $7.25 federal hourly minimum. The City Council of Seattle unanmiously voted to raise the minimum wage to $15 an hour. The city of Washington looks set to pass a $12.50 an hour rate in the coming weeks. And President Barack Obama has said he would support legislation to take the federal level to $10.10 an hour and thereafter link it to inflation.

The arguments in favor of a significantly higher U.S. minimum wage are strong. First, it would inject a much-needed stimulus into the anemic recovery without involving a dollar of taxpayer money. The economic case is also solid...higher minimum wages should not lead to higher unemployment. Copious research shows that a reasonable increase boosts employee loyalty, which reduces turnover and improves the company's bottom line. In addition, it boosts local consumer spending, which lifts business revenues. By large margins both Republicans and Democrats support raising the minimum wage, according to opinion polls.

> "The plutocrats are shamelessly autocratic and greed-obsessed, and believe themselves to be chosen by God to rule our lives. But they are blind to the consequences of their power-hungry policies. When the tipping point has been reached, revolutionary fervor and solutions can work their political magic... There are 1% of the plutocrats, and 99% of their victims. And those put-upon citizens are angry and know their pitchforks."
> – Bernard Weiner

A presidential election in the United States is always remarkable to behold – and 2016 more than ever. This is not just because America remains the world's only superpower, with unparalleled global military might. It is also because America is heading for one of its most uncertain national polls in decades, one set to be dominated by public anger over income inequality and cronyism in government.

"The share of voters who identify as independents, rather than Democrats or Republicans, recently hit an all-time high of 42 percent, according to Gallup. This is bad news for established figures in either party...Hillary Clinton should beware. So should Jeb Bush," warns Financial Times' Washington columnist Edward Luce

The sudden emergence center stage of a political party formed by principled progressives and conscientious conservatives would open up the debate to new ideas. For instance, they could put forth a common sense approach to reduce the deficit: cut military spending in half, initiate a financial transactions (Robin Hood) tax to reign in casino capitalism and raise the $113,700 payroll tax limit.

What are we waiting for? How long are we going to sit idly by and watch the political warmongers deploy their drones, their warships, their stealth bombers, their missiles, our sons and daughters, and ultimately, their nuclear weapons against the most impoverished peoples of the world? How long are we doing to ignore the corporate warmongers as they wield their magic profit wands that fill their wallets and bellies to overflowing while millions of children perish from hunger and preventable disease? How long are we going to accept the unjust equality of the 1% pocketing a grossly disproportionate amount of the wealth generated by the toil of the 99%? How long are we going to passively accept the suicidal insanity of raping and plundering our planet's finite resources to the point that none of us will be able to survive?

Let the Revolution begin!

APPENDIX

This pamphlet contains dozens of bits and pieces of other writers' work, remixed to make a point about some of the most relevant and difficult issues of the day. We wanted to expose the anti-democratic forces threatening America – and the world – by appropriating their thought-provoking reporting and commentary, occasionally overlaid with our own imagined scenarios. The following is a list of citations to the best of our recollection.

Numbers refer to pages:

xi

The truly profound change....Sheldon S. Wolin, *Democracy Incorporated: Managed Democracy and the Specter of Inverted Totalitarianism*

After 30 years of a market-driven immorality...Henry A. Giroux, "Intellectuals as Subjects and Objects of Violence," *Truthout*

1

Power is a far more complex...various, though probably from Edward R. Tufte, *The Cognitive Style of Powerpoint: Pitching Out Corrupts Within*

2

Today's American Society is the legacy...Christopher Caldwell, "At last, Snowden is causing an outrage," *Financial Times*

An extremely perilous development in U.S. politics...Bob Wing, "Rightwing Neo-Secession or a Third Reconstruction?" *Counterpunch*

In one of the most astounding acts of legerdemain in US history...John Atcheson, "Government Works Fine, Just Not For You," *Common Dreams*

3

In fact, there is a great deal one person...Gar Alperovitz and Keane Bhatt, "What Then Can I Do? Ten Ways to Democratize the Economy," *Truthout*

4

Americans are so frustrated with government... John Nichols and Robert McChesney, "Progressives Ask for Too Little, Not Too Much in Age of Plutocratic Rule," *Truthout*

5

The wealthy have installed their slaves...Stephane Hessel, *Time for Outrage*

In the late 1960s and early 1970s...Nichols and McChesney

6
A small group of U.S. institutions select...Wolin

7
The US, a country with a vast nuclear weapons...Paul Craig Roberts, "Obama Has Decided That It Is Safer To Buy Congress Than To Go It Alone"

Wall Street uses economic power backed...Rob Urie, "Capitalism and US Geopolitics," *Counterpunch*

In fact it is highly probable that the 2008...Gui Rochat, "Where Empires Fail," *The Greanville Post*

8
Threats to financial hegemony by such as...Rochat

The most deadly weapons of mass destruction...Garry Leech, "Let the Revolution Begin," *Counterpunch*

Sentence about Wall Street fraud...Lynn Stuart Parramore, "Wall Street Predators Wage Secret War on American Retirements," *AlterNet*

9
For American elites one of the longest...citation exists but we can't find it

11
The task of elitism in the so-called age...Wolin

The intense pace of work and the extended...Wolin

13
Having brought the world economy to...Martin Wolf, "Failing elites threaten our future," *Financial Times*

If the corporate politicians have no answers...Mark Vorpahl, *Workers Action*

15
Journalism is at a momentous crossroads...Norman Solomon, "Journalism at the Crossroads," *Counterpunch*

From the false Tonkin Gulf narrative...Solomon, "What the Assault on Whistleblowers Has to Do With War on Syria," *Common Dreams*

Democracy and accountable government...Roberts, "What Is The Real Agenda Of The American Police State?

Official Washington and the mainstream...Robert Parry, "Deceiving the US Public on Syria," *Consortiumnews*

16
The role of independent media is to tell...Noam Chomsky, "Media Control and the Indoctrination of the Unites States," *Truthout*

17
Real journalism is "subversive" of...Solomon

19
Business leaders and their elected friends...Richard Wolff, "Recovery hype: American capitalism's weapon of mass destruction," *The Guardian*

The Lehman Brothers crisis triggered...Gillian Tett, "Insane financial system lives post-Lehman," *Financial Times*

There's a huge resentment on the...Amy B Dean, "Will the Tea Party Pay for the Shutdown?" *Truthout*

For the last ten years, according to...Mel King and Rev. William Alberts, Ph.D., "The Best and Worse of 'Boston Strong,'" *Counterpunch*

20
What is wrong with the economy...Ted Rall, "Why Are Americans So Passive? Get Pissed Off and Break Things," *World News Daily*

A left-right alliance is extremely...Sam Husseini, "The Perennial 'Unusual' Yet Somehow Ubiquitous Left-Right Alliance," *Counterpunch*

In fact, it would be perfectly possible...Jean Bricmont, "The Wishful Thinking Left," *Counterpunch*

21
On issue after issue – taxes, the...Robert Borosage,"Populism Rising?" *Campaign for America's Future*

23
America's Tea Party is a rising of...John Kay, "Sinister or silly, protest politicians are united in grievance," *Financial Times*

Tea Partiers, like many Americans...Edward Luce, "It is stupid to believe that the Tea Party has no brain," *Financial Times*

24
Tea Partiers detest all things big:...Beth Rowan, "History of the Tea Party Movement," *infoplease*

25
What Tea Party activists have...John Sommers II, "Decision time for Tea Party movement in U.S. political contests," *Reuters*

The Tea Party caucus in Congress... Parramore, "Guilty of Sedition? Tea Party Threatens America's Economic and Political Systems," *AlterNet*

27
The middle classes have been on...First two sentences: Francis Fukuyama, "The Middle-Class Revolution," *The Wall Street Journal*; the rest is Parramore "Guilty..."

For good or ill, the Occupy movements..."What's There to Hope For? A Plague on Both Parties!" *LiveLeak*

The success of the "new left"...Thomas Pynchon, introduction to *Slow Learner*

Later many activist groups demanded...Charles Haymarket, "Why a Left movement Has Never Really Happened," *Counterpunch*

28
This moral superiority that is peculiar...First sentence is Russell Brand on revolution: "We no longer have the luxury of tradition"; third sentence: Parramore, "Novelist of the 99% is trending big-time as U.S. sinks into Dickensian nightmare," *AlterNet*

The conservative era will be brought...Thomas Frank, "To the Precinct Station," *The Baffler*

What should the left do? First of all...Bricmont

29
The question that remains is how can...Giroux, "The Ghost of Authoritarianism in the Age of the Shutdown," *Truthout*

31
Structural factors in the U.S. election..."Boehner And McConnell Have Primary Challenges – Why Not Steny Hoyer, Steve Israel And Debbie Wasserman Schultz?" *Before It's News*

Before votes are ever counted, money...Elliot Sperber, "Russell Brand and the Need for Planetary Adjustment," *Counterpunch*

Yet polls say a majority of voters are...Richard Eskow, "Debunking the Spin: Voters Want Change, Not 'Centrism,'" *Campaign for America's Future*

Amid the latest government shutdown...Jeffrey M. Jones, "In U.S., Perceived Need for Third Party Reaches New High," *Gallup*

32
To become powerful enough to transform...Vorpahl

The party has to represent a populist...First two sentences: Vorpahl

34
We know that we live...Robert Borosage, "Can Democracy Tame Plutocracy," *Campaign for America's Future*

35
As the Obama era nears its final midterm...Ken Thomas and Steve Peoples, "Contrast For Parties In 2016 Presidential Race," *AP*

38
The sentence: What America lacks is a figure... Mike Lofgren, "Anatomy of the Deep State: Beneath Veneer of Democracy, The Permanent Ruling Class," *Common Dreams*

41
Democracy is about the conditions that...Giroux, "Democracy and the Threat of Authoritarianism: Politics Beyond Barack Obama," *Truthout*

The kind of democracy that now envelopes...Mark Mazower, "The future of democracy," *Financial Times*

No one who lives under constant surveillance...Chris Hedges, "Our Sinister Dual State," *Truthdig*

Full Medicare for all, cracking down on...Ralph Nader, "The Dynastic Hillary Bandwagon – Bad for America," *The Nader Page*

When a state-corporate nexus of power...George Monbiot, "It's business that really rules us now," *The Guardian*

43
There is a new normal in America:...William J. Astore, "The Business of America Is War," *TomDispatch*

45
Stop counting carrier fleets, fighter jets...Philip Stephens, "Trade trumps missiles in today's global power plays," *Financial Times*

The collapse of the Soviet Union...Roberts, "As Ye Sow, So Shall Ye Reap"

46
Instead, influenced by neoconservative...Roberts

47
Ordinary folks, the 99%, don't have...Bill Gross, "Scrooge McDucks," *PIMCO*

The super rich want the homeless to...Paul Buchheit, "The 8 Groups in America That Are the Most Screwed-Over by Predatory Capitalism," *AlterNet*

With the "financialization" of the...CJ Polychoniou, "The Political Economy of Predatory Capitalism," *Truthout*

In January 2013 Fix the Debt...Mary Bottari, "Erskin Bowles and Alan Simpson Reach New Heights of Hypocrisy in 'Fix the Debt' Ad," *PRWatch*

Americans are very clear. They don't...Dean

48
Most of the poverty in the United States...Lawrence Davidson, "The Mind of the Poor," *World News Daily*

49
Most bank lending today does not...Dirk Bezemer, "Big finance is a problem, not an industry to be nurtured," *Financial Times*

Business tax cuts don't create many...Jack Rasmus, "The Contradictions of Global Fiscal-Monetary Policy," *Counterpunch*

Big business and finance capital...Polychroniou

51
Our adventure on Earth...Hessel

We are in the midst of economic...Jomo KwameSundaram, "A Global Green New Deal for Sustainable Development," *Inter Press Service*

When scientists at Mauna Loa Observatory...Richard Smith, "Sleepwalking to Extinction," *Adbusters*

According to new research, the debate...Jon Queally, "'We Believe!' Even Reddest States Admit Climate Change Real," *Common Dreams*

52
Carbon concentrations have not been...Smith

The world's climate scientists tell us...Smith

53
We all know what we have to do:...Smith

This doesn't mean we would have...Smith

54
The ongoing disaster at the Daichi...Amy Goodman, "Fukushima: An Ongoing Warning to the World," *Democracy Now!*

We may be fast approaching the...Smith

55
We all know the world is in big...William Bloom, "Team Obama/Cult Obama"

Change often happens by making...Rebecca Solnit, "Victories Come in All Sizes," *TomDispatch*

As the government's powers of...Michael Ignatieff, "Free polarized politics from its intellectual vacuum," *Financial Times*

56
What is missing are those alternative...Giroux interviewed by Bill Moyers, *Mloyers & Company*

The right since the 1970s has created...Moyers, "Henry Giroux: Zombie Politics and Casino Capitalism," *Truthout*

The large social movements on the left...Giroux, "The Violence of Organized Forgetting," *Truthout*

How to keep the issue of inequality...Except for the first sentence: Dean

57
In the past few months, American...Luce, "A higher minimum wage is the tonic America needs," *Financial Times*

The arguments in favor of a significantly...Luce

58
What are we waiting for?...Leech

ABOUT THE AUTHORS

ALAN SUTTON is a philanthropist, filmmaker and writer living in Southern California. Sutton is the Executive Producer of the feature documentary *The Manzanar Fishing Club* and co-wrote the non-fiction book *Jeet Kune Do: The Art and Philosophy of Bruce Lee.* Sutton was a senior marketing and distribution executive at Universal Pictures before retiring in 2008.

REX YOSHIMOTO is a freelance writer living in Bellingham, Washington. A veteran of the Vietnam War, he is the author of the novel *The Crows Under The Dragon's Wing.*